Contents

KU-713-996

You are important.
You need to stay safe.

Stay Safe!

80 002 886 667

Your Own Safety

Sue Barraclough

www.heinemann.co.uk/library

Visit our website to find out more information about Heinemann Library books.

To order:
- ☎ Phone 44 (0) 1865 888066
- 🗎 Send a fax to 44 (0) 1865 314091
- 💻 Visit the Heinemann Bookshop at www.heinemann.co.uk/library to browse our catalogue and order online.

First published in Great Britain by Heinemann Library, Halley Court, Jordan Hill, Oxford OX2 8EJ, part of Pearson Education. Heinemann is a registered trademark of Pearson Education Ltd.

© Pearson Education Ltd 2008
First published in paperback in 2008
The moral right of the proprietor has been asserted.

All rights reserved. No part of this publication may be reproduced, stored in a retrieval system, or transmitted in any form or by any means, electronic, mechanical, photocopying, recording, or otherwise, without either the prior written permission of the publishers or a licence permitting restricted copying in the United Kingdom issued by the Copyright Licensing Agency Ltd, 90 Tottenham Court Road, London W1T 4LP (www.cla.co.uk).

Editorial: Diyan Leake and Cassie Mayer
Design: Joanna Hinton-Malivoire
Illustration: Paula Knight
Picture research: Erica Martin
Production: Duncan Gilbert

Origination by Chroma Graphics (Overseas) Pte Ltd
Printed and bound in China by South China Printing Co. Ltd

ISBN 978 0 431 18437 1 (hardback)
12 11 10 09 08
10 9 8 7 6 5 4 3 2 1

ISBN 978 0 431 18444 9 (paperback)
12 11 10 09 08
10 9 8 7 6 5 4 3 2 1

British Library Cataloguing in Publication Data
Barraclough, Sue
  Your own safety. - (Stay safe!)
  1. Accidents - Prevention - Juvenile literature 2. Offenses against the person - Prevention - Juvenile literature
  3. Safety education - Juvenile literature
  I. Title
  613.6

Acknowledgements
The publishers would like to thank Sister Patty Fillenworth for assistance in the preparation of this book.

Every effort has been made to contact copyright holders of any material reproduced in this book. Any omissions will be rectified in subsequent printings if notice is given to the publishers.

Northamptonshire Libraries & Information Service	
80 002 886 667	
Peters	07-Jul-2008
363.1	£5.25

Do you know how to keep yourself safe?

Never stay on your own with someone you do not know very well.

Always stay with friends, parents, or teachers.

Never do anything that makes you feel unsafe.

8

Always say: "No!" if anything
feels unsafe.
Trust your feelings.

Never go with anybody if it has not been planned.

Always know who is collecting
you from school.
Check with a parent or teacher.

11

Never do what a stranger asks you.

Always say: "No," if a stranger asks you to come along.
Find a parent or teacher to help you.

Never help a stranger.

Always tell strangers to ask a grown-up for help if they need it.

Never take presents from someone
you do not know well.

Always say: "No, thank you".

Never stay where you feel unsafe.
Do not go with anybody that you do
not know.

Always go to someone in charge to ask for help.

Always know your address.

Always know your phone number.

Always remember these safety rules and you will stay safe.

Rules for keeping yourself safe

- Stay together with friends, parents, or teachers.
- Trust your feelings about staying safe.
- Always know who is collecting you from school.
- Say, "No," if a stranger asks you to come along.
- Tell strangers to ask a grown-up for help.
- Say, "No, thank you," if a stranger gives you presents.
- Go to someone in charge to ask for help.
- Know your address and phone number.

Picture glossary

 **feeling** something that you feel inside

 **stranger** person you do not know

 **trust** believe that something is right

Index

Notes for parents and teachers

Before reading

Ask the children who keeps them safe (parents, friends, teachers, childminders, police). Talk about how these people help, such as by taking them to school, collecting them from school, looking after them at home, when shopping, or helping them if they are lost.

After reading

Safety Steps. Stand the children in a line and explain they can take a step forward if what you say is safe but they must stand still if what you say is not safe. Watch the children and make them take two steps backwards if they make a mistake that is dangerous. For example: "Step forward if it is safe if your parents collect you from school ... if a stranger asks you to get in the car ... if a stranger asks you to help ... if your grandparents give you a present ..."

Home circle. Teach the children their home telephone number and address. Encourage them to say their house number and first line of their address. If they know it, invite them to join in a circle. Repeat with telephone numbers. Note those children who are still uncertain and encourage them to learn the details to join in the circle.